MW01639982
PHONE LINE
IN
OUT
ON
OFF

Use my tail for a bookmark!

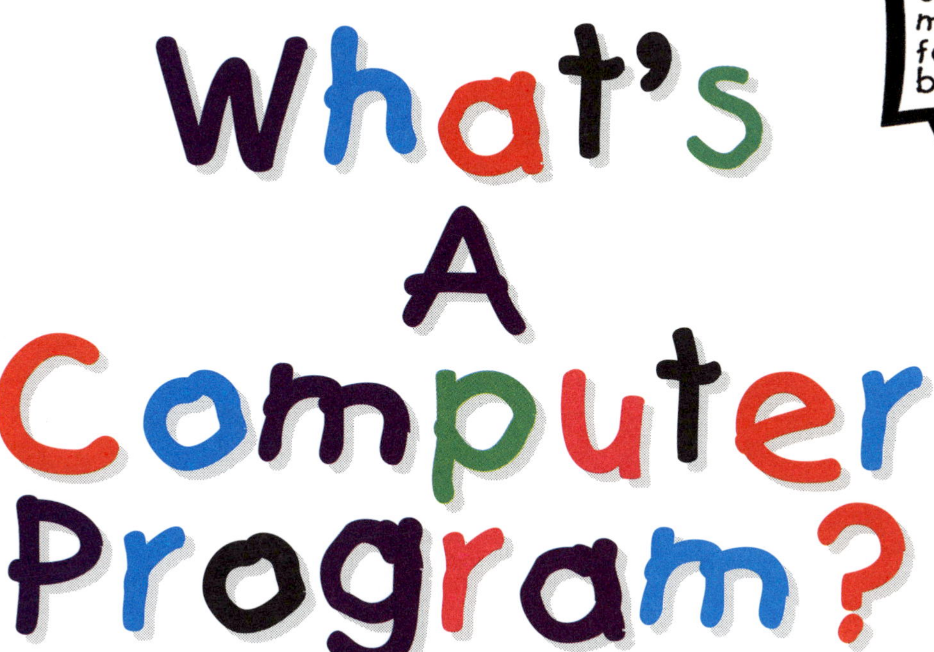

Words by Edna Toby & Bob Stevens
Drawings by Bob Stevens

For Debra, Lori, Michelle
Norma and David

Library of Congress Cataloging-in-Publication Data

Toby, Edna, 1942-
What's a computer program? / words by Edna Toby & Bob Stevens : drawings by Bob Stevens.
p. cm.
Includes Index.
Summary: A simple introduction to computer software and applications, related vocabulary, trivia facts, and a story about computer uses.
ISBN 0-9662813-2-2 (hardcover)
1. Computer programs--Juvenile Literature. [1. Computer programs.]
I. Stevens, Bob 1948- . II. Title.
QA76.23.T64 1998
005--dc21 98-3244
CIP
AC

First published in the United States by
New Traditions Press, Inc.
Post Office Box 1567 Gracie Station
New York City, NY 10028

Printed in Singapore

What's A Computer Program?

A **Computer Program** is special instructions that teach your **Computer** how to do a particular job. It's like sending your **Computer** to school.

Two other words for **Program** are **Application** and **Software**.

In a quiet corner of the forest stands a cozy little cottage. It's the home of the Mouse Family, Mom, Dad, Junior and Baby.

Junior watched Mom and Dad using their **Computer**.

"What are you working on, Pop?"

"Some family vacation plans. Then Baby can have a turn on the Computer."

"And you, Mom?"

"I brought home a little work from the office."

All computers understand the same language. It's called BINARY or MACHINE LANGUAGE.

Junior was amazed at how many different jobs the **Computer** could do.

"Different **Programs** let your **Computer** do different things." Dad explained. "The information you put into or take out of your **Computer** is called **Data**."

"Documents are the paintings, songs, stories and poems you make with your Programs."

Anything you make with a Program is called a Document.

Computers are made in factories. The first factories were built in England about 225 years ago. They were used to make cloth from cotton.

When **Software** is put into your **Computer**, it's called **Installing Software.**

The Operating System or OS for short, is Software Installed at the factory. It lets your Computer understand the Commands you give it and keeps it running smoothly.

When you give your **Computer** an order, it's called a **Command**.

"Here are some useful **Commands**."

The **Save Command** protects your work.

The **Print Command** lets you see your work on paper.

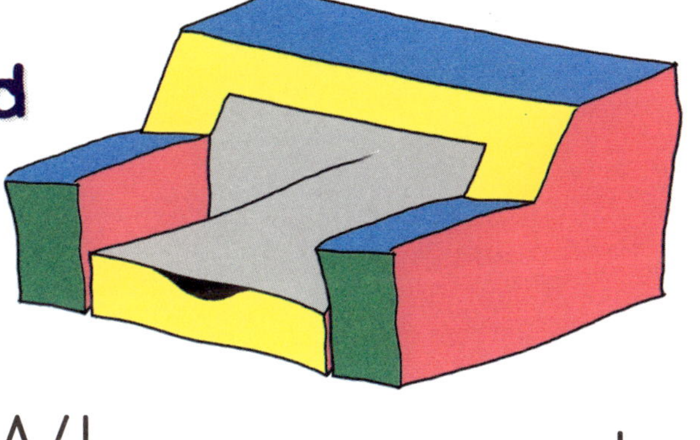

When you want to work on something again use the **Open Command**.

"I want to use my Computer to paint a picture of our house. Is there a Command for that?"

"No, son. To paint with your Computer you need a Painting Program."

Working With Pictures

To create works of art, use the pencils, paint brushes, buckets, different color paints, erasers, and spray cans, in your **Painting Program**.

Leonardo da Vinci painted the Mona Lisa in the year 1506. He used oil paints on a wood panel...not a computer.

Use circles, squares, rectangles, lines and triangles to build a picture in your **Drawing Program**.

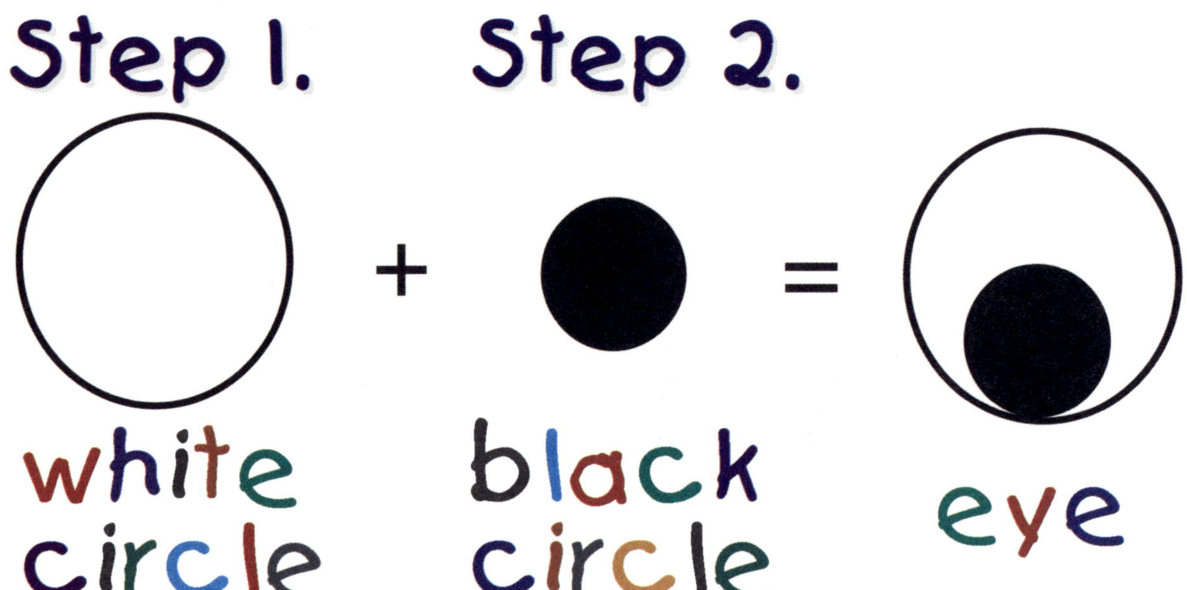

Working With Words

CD-ROM Story Books read to you.

To make things happen **Click** on the pictures. **Clicking** is when you press the button on your **Mouse**.

A **Word Processor** lets you write down your ideas.

You can change how your ideas look by changing the **Fonts** you use. A **Font** is a group of letters and numbers that look the same.

Other ways of changing how your ideas look are by using color, underlining, adding punctuation marks, and using pictures.

FONTS

FUN!

WORKING WITH NUMBERS

Collect all your friend's addresses
and phone numbers
in a **Database Program.**

Why do the hands on a clocks move clockwise?

Tell time with a **Computer Clock**. Keep track of your allowance with a **Spreadsheet**. Use a **Calculator** to add and subtract. Look up your birthday with a **Calendar Program**.

The first clocks were made to move the way a shadow moves around the face of a sun dial.

Working With Sounds

A **Music Application** let's you write songs and hear your music. You can record sounds with a **Microphone** .

Born in 1770, Ludwig von Beethoven was one of the greatest composers that ever lived. He was totally deaf.

Playing Games

Your **Computer** is the most awesome game machine ever invented. Escape from Dundor and save the world.

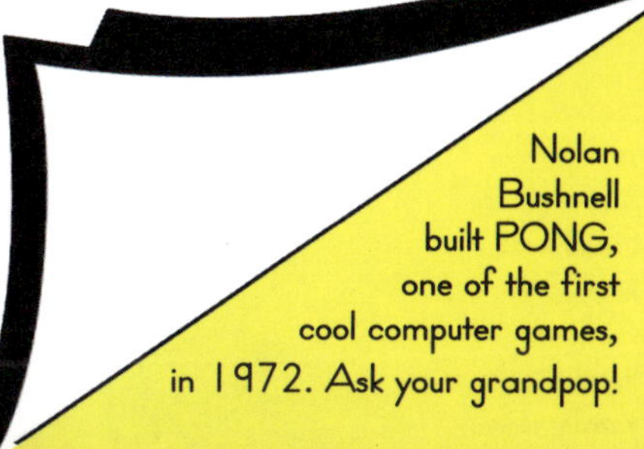

Using Other Programs

Build a bird house, make pretty clothing for your dolls and collect stamps with **Hobby Applications.**

Screen Savers are fun Programs that have the serious job of protecting your Monitor's Screen.

Design a beautiful quilt with Craft Software.

Explore far away places using **Internet Software.**

The world's first encyclopedia was written 2,368 years ago in ancient Greece. It was written by a man named Speusippus.

Learn everything,
about anything,
with a **Computer Encyclopedia.**

"Do you still want to paint a picture of our home, Son?"

"Sure! But now I think I'll add the sounds of the forest, and make it a calendar. Then I'll write a poem with my **Word Processor**. I'll send it to all my friends using their addresses in my **Database**. I can even send it to my buddies in Africa and Asia over the **Internet**. What do you think, Pop?"

"Sounds great! I bet it would make a good **Screen Saver** too."

Junior was ready to get down to work.

WORKING SMART

Keep your disks safe. Heat, dirt and liquids can damage them.

Many **Programs** come with helpful information built into them.

Sometimes a **Program** stops working. That's called **Crashing** or **Freezing**. It's not your fault. Ask a grownup for help.

Pretty boxes can fool you. Don't waste your money. Buy what you need.

You can learn about new **Software** from your parents, in magazines and books, at **Computer** stores, from friends, and on the **Internet**.

Programs come with a **Manual**. A **Manual** is a book that tells you how to use the **Application**.

Glossary/Index

Application	page 3	Instructions that tell your computer how to do a particular job. It's another word for software or program.
Binary	page 6	The language all computers understand.
CD-ROM	page 15	A small round disk that holds data.
Command	page 9	An order you give to your computer.
Computer	page 3	An information factory.
Computer Encyclopedia	page 25	A database of knowledge.
Crashing/ Freezing	page 28	When your computer jams up and has to be restarted.
Data	page 6	Another word for information.
Database	page 18	Special software that organizes information like names or phone numbers.
Document	page 7	Computer talk for something you make with a program like a painting or a song.
Drawing Program	page 14	An application that builds works of art using objects like squares, circles, and triangles.
Font	page 16	A group of letters and numbers that all look the same.
Input Device	page 30	Something you use to put information into your computer like a microphone or a key– board.
Installing Software	page 8	When a program is put into your computer.
Machine Language	page 6	The language all computers understand same another term for BINARY.

Manual	page 29	An instruction book.
Microphone	page 20	An input device, you use to put sounds into a computer. (See Input Device.)
Monitor	page 23	An output device that shows your work. (See Output Device.)
Open Command	page 11	An order to work on a document again.
Operating System	page 9	Software that runs your computer.
OS	page 9	Short for Operating System.
Output Device	page 30	Something we use to get information out of our computer like a monitor or printer.
Painting Program	page 13	An application for creating works of art.
Print Command	page 11	An order to send your work to the printer.
Program	page 3	Instructions that tell your computer how to do a particular job. It's another word for application or software.
Save Command	page 11	An order to keep your work for another time.
Screen	page 23	The part of a monitor that shows your work.
Screen Saver	page 23	A program that keeps your monitor screen safe.
Software	page 3	Instructions that tell your computer how to do a particular job. It's another word for application or program.
Spreadsheet	page 19	A program that helps you work with numbers.
Story Book	page 15	A program that reads stories to you.
Word Processor	page 16	A program that helps you write stuff.

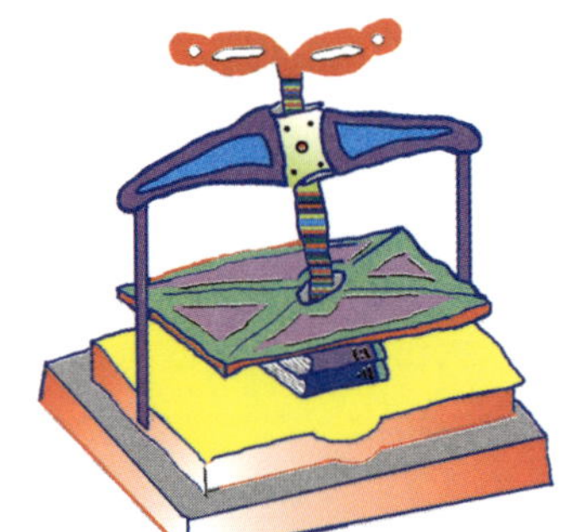

New Traditions Press Inc.

P. O. Box 388 Ashland OH 44805

"The coolest, smartest stuff you'll find on any kid's bookshelf."

Phone, Fax Or Mail Your Order Today!

Phone 1.800.247.6553 - Fax 1.419.281.6883

Visit us at www.bookmasters.com

What's A Computer? How many @19.95? ☐ ______

What's The Internet? How many @19.95? ☐ ______

What's A Computer Program? How many @19.95? ☐ ______

Special Deal!!!! How many @49.95? ☐ ______

Buy all three great books for the special price of $49.95!

Shipping & Handling 3.95

Subtotal ______

OH residents add 6% sales tax ______

NY residents add 8¼% sales tax ______

Total ______

Visa ☐ MC ☐ Discovery ☐

______ name on card

______ card number ______ exp. date

Photocopy this form and mail or fax your order to us today!

PHONE LINE
IN OUT
ON OFF